UNLIMITED BRANCHES
OF DIFFERENCE

Khari Thompson

Inquiries and Book Orders should be addressed to:

Great Writers Media
Email: info@greatwritersmedia.com
Phone: 877-600-5469

ISBN: 978-1-961416-50-5 (sc)
ISBN: 978-1-961416-51-2 (ebk)

FOREWARD

I wrote this without using an inch of my own ability. I am schizo-phrenic and sometimes voices do unexplainably kind things, like making poetry pour from my fingers. This entire book is thanks to a nameless voice. I am not the person I was before, not trapped in a deafening universe, not isolated beyond belief, or coming up with the intentions of God with his universe. My whole life I have been the voice. It does as it pleases and I simply, well, it has shown me that I do not exist. It placed my consciousness in my legs and moved my body and lips and vocal chords without my permission. I am some-thing, definitely, but it is clear that the voice is more. This book of poetry is about me, definitely. It is about my life shaded by imagery. I am in every one of these poems, and maybe you are too. Intensely human, these poems catalogue my very mundane experiences in a way that reeks of too much of everything, a very ladeness that has been called "galactic". I am trying my very best, and the things I do are all in that vein.

Special thanks to my grandmother who believed in me and made it possible to make this book be published.

Being Good Friends

Wind ruins
So many things,
Where people are variables
And kindness is
An operator

Nothing gets in
Between two
People like wind,
The flying point
Of access for the
Brisk cold,
And the extreme warmth
That needs someone in
A jacket
To doff their protection
To let it step
Over
A cloud's puddles
With two
People, between them is
The street sweeper,
The tongue of an energetic
Speaker that
Blows her
Hot air strongly, two
Ways at once.

So far
From revival,
Wind has nothing
To hold, and everything falls

Through it,
Until friends
Stand in the way
Long enough for
Speeds to increase
And foundations of the
Heart to
Perforate

A rolling ball has
More control
Than two people
In the face of the wind
However, wind can
Be harnessed,
It can be taught
To behave.
Once one masters the
Idea of relating
Underwater,
A stroke of reduced neuroticism
And a reduction of force.

Force and
Wind bled together
In war,
And through
The oral contraption
We see internalized
Windfulness,
As small hiccups of
Energetic directionality escape
The human mouth.

It is the wind,
Outside and inside,
Always outside, briefly inside,
That corners us, so deeply, while
We're putting ourselves into
A locked position
On the floor
With our friend.
Wind is responsible
For the determination
That we cannot
Stand one another,
And when we press
The wind out of our aquafers
We realize the true
Way to fill our lungs
Is with water,
Because to share this water,
Inside and out,
Is to give the gift of life.

We will not tear with water.
We will say only good things
When each breath is a gulp.
Blooming in preciousness
Is to consider that we have
Only moments to
Share what we'd like,
No force,
No unending resource through
Which hurricanes may happen;
Instead a severe lashing that
Takes off fat, a gurgling
Output that heightens our present,
A solo act that extends graciousness

To this limited capacity to speak,
And a running of constant downward
movement that forms our waterfall
Of peaceful short-turned words

This is why wind
Is everywhere, and water
is concentrated.
To your friend,
Have only limited,
Life-giving options
Escape from the gasping
Pulsar that is
Hewn from
Our replacement of
Ubiquity with scarcity.

When We Disagree

On the run
With several buttons
Fastening candied
Agreements on the
Undercarriage of
My displeasure

I am unable to see that
My turkey wings fold;
I eat out at times
When the last bird
Will carry me to
Its home

I am drastic for this,
Portraying light sodas
In my gestures
Of gratitude

In the system there
Are agreements; on
Nothing but trees
I beam the beam
Of four
To six arguments

It's time to
Draw the line

Over a piece
Of dramatic land,
I retract my wing
And finally know
What was unreachable.

I am so
Stubborn like that,
And without
Peace,
I am so glad
That we
Stayed here this
Long

Praise be to dinosaur wings;
They were the progenitor
Of my condition,
And then I split
My way
Into four
Or six
Dimensions—
Each to be known by
A severe drawback of the hand

Kiss me,
Treat the sky with
My armor,
And surprise the
Gleam with a
Gleam

Goodnight all,
For now is
The position of
Ravens
Receiving their
Soda, and the rivalry of
The night is done.

It Grows Backwards

With a boiling sense
Of overwork,
They prescribe donuts
Into our blood,
Only ever encouraging
Signs of a disturbed mechanical spring,
Like how underneath the pressure
We can only taste like the
Dazzling fortunes that
Meld into candy

It's prescribed
That in the last
Days, we will eat
Our own timeline,
That the drip
Of continuance
Will create
A
Boulder
Inside of our
Willingness
To jump ahead and defeat
The coldest
Actuarial judgments

It's some summer stuff
That later in the year we learned
How to fold into a hat.
This is the only place

Where we can harness
Our true ancient
Feelings,
The ones that
Only
Came about just
Now, but
exist in a
Network of vacuum-
Sealed containers,
Where they
Have grown for
Three hundred thousand
Lifetimes

I will not have weird
Screwing
Up this
Trip,
And I will pay
The Nordic price for
Destroying fate

I am so tired
Of the grains that pass us
In a vertical manner,
Because sand was scarce—
A waste—
And then every movement forward
Had a brim like our hat

And I am so sick
Of the land that is
Ingrown in your
Forehead,
To be settled by
People who settled
A foreign mind years
Ago;
But I feel that
The bright color of
Doing what has been done
Is it not
Being done, and,
Under the guise
Of melding nights,
The passage of time
Licked the settlers
And left them anew.

This I know.

We are taking our
Time,
And seeking
Only what comes
About after
Walking in a straight line,
Which has its merit
Like the bird wing does,
But not like pizza does...
And this is what wrecks
My forward moving inertial
Drive.

So time
Must give us
A reason
To understand,
Instead of showing
Us the rote
Actions of what is to be done
(The way it is
Done when
We imagine
Our futures)
And we have to give back
A mind
Every time we
Take a
Breath.
It's worth it.

She Has To Stop

A food type
Brings lots of joy
To you harmoniously
With the other animals
You keep under
Your garment

The shame won
The case,
But you generously gave
In the
Hardwood kitchen
Where we egged on
The jury

I don't regret our actions;
It's like, without you,
There would be no beat—
Your esophagus
Keeps time as you compress your
morals—a precious
Piece of a trance
That lulls us away from
Our portions

I am without defense
When I come over,
And then, when
You come over,
There's less
Fiber to rely
On

Every time
You put another item
Away, I leave
My dreaming behind
And ask the Lord
for more forks,
For I need them
To put
A stake in
What's right.
If only you
Would feed it
To your animals,
And leave
The world alone.

The torque
In my love
For you is
Directly
Proportional to your
Self-control, and
Inside of it
There's a direct-proportion
To that control that you lack.
Both manage time
And the wave augments,
Which gives me hope
That I will one day
Eat in your
Presence.

Dreams Only Prawns Can See

Blisters are
Singing.
There's
Nothing like a
Protocol
In the deep South,
Where voices collide with
Sugar, converted
To
Boils underneath my
Skin

I do not want
To blast off. I never
Want to leave, and that's
How I ended up
With a prison cell
Hanging from my neck—fashion.

And then
I asked a
Belle for
Her name, and of course,
There was
Nothing I
Could say when she
Told me,
"You are dreaming
Again",
Although then I pinched
My friend
And he said "ow". I don't
believe I

Could've
Done anything else, in
That moment

And then, after every sound
Had pierced my cavernous
Ear, I positioned
A little bit of
Courage so that
I could challenge
Her on her own
Dream theory,
With words that came from
Talismans given
To me by a
Naked goon

It's never
Too late to swim through your
Blessings; unfortunately
They are drawn in colors
That only prawns can
See, like
The way I
Asked her if
I could be
Dreaming if the
Time was 7:00. Things
Like this assert reality,
And she would never be
Right for disagreeing.

There were others, as well
Tight people in Tight outfits
That wanted
Me to know

That I was not alive.
And then I, of course,
Licked the
Appropriate actor
To activate his
Skin's properties—the
Meld and the hold, which
Kept me together
With the
Actions he would take.
And from then on
I was flying, like
Him.
The belle was wrong.

It's not a
Lot, no. Under
The breath of
A genie, I
Had another chance, another
Choice.
Forgetting her I
Sampled lakewater
And it tasted like
A barrel of crabs. This
Was real—crabs live in water.
In the time
That I spent
On Earth, I
Learned, energetically,
That there is no
Such thing as
A dream.

This is the only thing I know.

And then I watched the crown
Drop upon my head
And knew that I would
Never wake up
Or go to sleep,
Or drift along in a semi-somnia or
Half-awake.
I am here, and while I am
Here,
There is
More value
In staying as I am than
There is betraying the actions
of God, as they happen, in
His physicsless mind.
Because why, I do
Not know, but what
is dreamlike about
The Deep South?

Stop Operating

The way
Your anger
Subsides
Is like a tube falling
Into
A trench. You
Don't understand—I have you
And that's
It.

I prefer facts
To cartridges; there is
Less to see and more to
Have. You are
Contained in a cartridge,
And my eyes wander.

There is nothing we can do
About your deep purple glow.
As a group we
Try
And turn you
Three degrees toward the moon,
but all we see is a planet
Turning
Tide-locked in orbit around
Us.

I am not
Trying to understand

You,
I'm just seeking a better hand.

This has to
Be the last
Original sentence
That you
Will spin
From your anger;
I wish
A piece
Of the
Seven Great Computer Programs
Would appear
For you to
Commiserate with,
Because you need it so

He can't
Be less of
A man
Who does this for you.
Capitalize my being
And we will see if
I can
Run this race in a more threatening
Outfit.

I am your boss.
Stop doing the things that
Jeopardize our workplace.

I wish everything about you
Was as
Sharp as
A lily's petal,
But ,
We can't
All have
The same diameter or
Width. I ask you to
Convert into
Something concrete
And final, to liquify your
Ancient wound.

Thank you in
Advance.

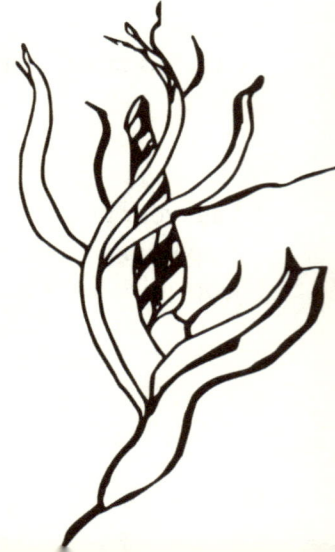

A Targeted Sup

A system has
Palates that only desire
Me and you put together
For a meal

It's not often
We polish the
Plate, but
Each time the food
Falls into our
Mouths
it eliminates a
Branch from our
Government

I can't seem to stop
Eating—
The only meaning
I can find when I try
Is hindered
By the
Dining room door

Tonight we will
Put our spoons
Together like Dance
Dance Revolution,
and the organized

Manner of our
Collection of
Moves
Will increase
The amount
Of consumption

Workday Today

My brains slip
Out of the
Cuff
Of my
Blazer.
There is no more time
For putty, so the more
Action I
Take the
Better
Suited I
Am
For form.

I request
For my
Braindead attitude to
Quit for
The day.
There are more rungs
To be read
About,
And it
Challenges my bias

Long gone, into
A period of sadness,
Like the
Way they
Dragged their

Plow. I am overcome
By the sound
Of the
Edge.

It's simple.
I will ask to say
"No". I
Could've
When my
Job cropped
My
Brain, making
It impossible for my
Hands to reach out to
The interminable.

Future hopefuls
Always seek me out. So
In winter I'll drop the
Ball. They
Will be drained
And I will
Expect
To speak

The figure
Whose arch
Spreads into the heighth
Will
Become coveted
By our company,
Because when things bend

They can break
And a vulnerable heart
Is one that can
Crack into
Cash

I will be no more beholden
To the edge of my
Ability than
A sitting doll is
To its
Recorded responses.

It's not in me to
Do things like this.
So I frown again,
And plunge my buttons
Onto my coat.

Try Harder

Sort of blue,
Kind of green, like
The original scales on
Steamed mermaid

I cast my voice loud
To catch a
Mermaid at a
High point in
Her life.
What is delicate desire
As it
Jettisons across
A deepend ocean? Convincing?
Vortices with quiet
Engorge themselves
On my sound;
Branches of
Water interweave
And sling around.
It's the
De-threading of my sonorous
Noise that upsets me,
Knitting my
Words into a sine
That sings
High and low
Notes
In a watery plane,
On a centripetal circle.

It is lost.

Dim as winter, the light
Portrays
The measure of my
Well-spent time.
I do not have
The energy of
The decorator;
I unknowingly
Push my words
Further out
Than I expected

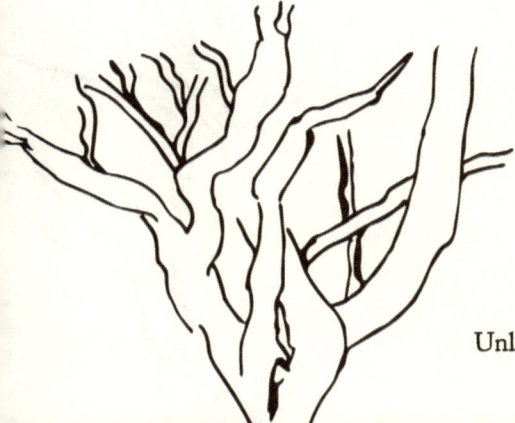

Netflix

So
I whisper to you
About the endings
You wanted to see
And receive feedback from
Swats, violent pats

It's only enough
If you tell me to stop,
Because words are
The progenitor to
Actions.

Seminary

A bit of orange
Is nice in the morning
A preacher, his words,
Looking bold into the sky
A picture like a salad

Smoking For A Moment

Over little bits i
Drive, lighting up
A cigarette when
I'm tired of breathing
To help rejuvenate
The need

I am
Defeating
A long time.
I turn my mind
Into a smaller adjective
That describes
This particular moment,
Honing in on a specific
Taste that
Drives me into the sun
Where I can light
My next cigarette

I am determined
To steam, to
Let my mind
Turn into an adjective
To describe this
Particular moment. I am
Not too tired
To appreciate that I
Am okay. The breath
That turns over
In my lungs

Is colored now
And I am defeating
A long time.

I am
Over the moon,
Behind several veneers
And still obtaining
Enough steam to
Quicken my pace
Through the same space
Over and over again,
Elongated circle,
Ellipse,
Trailing off into dots
That capsize and turn
Into moments. It is
Like a time well spent
That I understand
These opportunities
To let myself steam,
Pursuing something,
Never knowing what.
I am not confused
But simply expressing a
Moment in time.
Let's stay under
This top
Until the
Cigarette ends
And the butt
Gives way to
An extinguished universe.

Sandy Bits Of People, Places, And Things

An eager
Sand storm is
Never without its
Program of
Intent,
Never adding
A thing
To the informed
Mind that
Doesn't
Have roots
In silica
Made smaller
Through
Runs through
Water
And blades
Of wind

I am so sorrowful
About the
Lack of dreams
Inside of
The dream house,
Never told
About the
Ancient
Wounds that
Surround more
People than
A limited carousel

Operator's functioning
Inside of a pearly
Gatehouse

I am
Not taking
Things seriously
Anymore
Because the
Sand deposits
Whatever I
Need inside
Of me,
Making trinkets
Played like
Torpedoes
Into the original
Blanket
That laid over
The hard
Danger, Capital Danger,
That poured
Out no
Questionable
Receptacles
Into the
Drainage.
Only hard,
Indecipherable
Words that
Are the baskets
Which sit
Atop the
Anger I feel
At the

Disposition
Of the Sand

Because the
Sand has a
Disposition,
A way of being
That is taught
To it
By a
Corporeal
Bond
Between it and
The arteries
Of desert
It came from

I am sitting,
Legs folded,
And dreaming
A way for my eyes
To bench a
Thousand pounds,
So that when
The sand
Comes I am
Strong enough
To see my way through
It, not through it
But **through** it,
Until
I am illuminated
By what it has to
Offer.

I am not
Aching today
And that is
Not because of my
Joints
But because
Of the
Satisfaction
That comes with
Dunes,
A drenching
That encourages
Sloppy
Land to become
The only way
I know things.

The trembling
Of several talons
Overhangs my
Dreams,
As various
Birds migrate
To the sandy expanse
And pick out
With accuracy like
Domino numbers,
Taking their
Pick of whichever
Bit of flesh I
Have, ligamented
To the granules,
Until I
Remember something
That has something

To do with the
Fresh water
Demands of
The present moment.
It is like
This that
Gorges reverse
In my conversation
And I build
An even
Bridge everywhere
All at once
To what I need to yield

I am protected
In several forms
And do nothing
As honorable
Dunes
Rise and fall
In my breath
And air. I am
Seeing nothing,
Right now, that
My eyes
Don't want to
See and I am encouraged
Enough to tell you
What I need to say. This
Is never going to stop,
Even when I am old,
A piece of gratuitous labor
That enters
A being
That courses

With great knowledge
And spits up
What eventually
Will be avoided
By dogs
And eaten by
People.

The back
Of my head
Blisters
and I am sent to
A version of
Release.

Patent Perfect People

Oh,
How And When And Why
There are many things
And on top of that
There are
More things,
Like pieces
Standing in everyone's way
Drawing breath
From a toxicity
Of wonder,
A place
Of pure
Unadulterated
Understanding
Like ferocious planning
And wonderful
Agriculture

A bead of
Sweat makes
Every under
And over
And beside
Thing like
All other
Things,
And preaching
On top of
That is a slant
Of forest fire

That engulfs
The sand
And turns
Glass into
Mirrors
For us to become.

There is no other
Time that
Sits
With us,
No pondering
That could ever
Reduce
A blind
Quarter,
Never unseeing
The worth it has
But forever
Unknowing
And traipsing
Across
The bellyful
Mouths
Of several
Underserved
And unloved
Portrayers

There are
Things that
This universe
Doesn't want

Us to see,
And in that moment
We understand
That there has never been
A picture,
Only pictures,
Only things which
Will tie
The beginning
Up into a
Random set
Of push
Pull sets
And fringes

A portion
Of all Death
Happens when
We eat our
Words in a torrent
Of
Candlelight
And it's this
That positions
The demon
On our
Massive
And undersized
Protection
Order.
We are not
When or where,
how, why, an outcome
Or anything
That hasn't been

Untouched
In a way that
Seems lost
Through several
And more
Patents
That were performed,
Live,
In front of our sun.

Waiter! Waiter!

A hand
Presses against the
Lobster tail and
Upends the crab into the
Dessert bar like a wispy
Teenager

I ask him if he's done
And he proclaims that
Nothing is
Ever done, that
There is no attack
That comes without a
presence going
Before it into
An afterward that is sunken
Into a bottomless boil.

I am creased
And uncertain about
The iron; there is nothing
In this moment that
Could pry me from my
Furrow at the man's actions.
Why must you cause
A moment to occur,
Here, at this hour?
You are lost, sir,
In your own house of
Undoing, and there is
No waiter strong enough
To pry you from its throughput.

There is space
For other things
To rely on this moment,
But I end them with a bellow
For security.

For A Time, Deleted

The continued
Effort, drawing blank
Edges around
Something that should be
Done, a crafty attempt
At putting forth a foot,
With dreams dancing
About on the precipice
Like a mantel on a painted
Fireplace. I am not hot this time,
And the angels scream at me, blending
A bit of chastity with a dearth of overcome
Senses.

It is unreal
At the time of projection.
I cannot breathe more than I am
Supposed to in this disorganized
Land, and through it all I become hung
Over the bottom rail, the rack
Or the lantern that blazed through the
Night.
It is with stones that I create a clasp,
Asking the angels to bind me with fire,
And then demanding a pool
Open up at the foot of the mountain
For lizards to approach with their
Open-air beacon. I reach underneath
My anticipation and draw out
The few things I have left
To do things with, and then
My hand bleeds with constant anger,

Until I am unable to finish what I
Have started
Without balancing the correct
Anatomical model
Of the effort's skin.

The Last Few Years

The line,
Having been broken,
Has not had an even
Trace to the endpoint.
Always ending, the line
Produces us,
A buoy in the red green
Lights, almost stupendous
In that
Particular
Talisman which holds
Its whole
Body, letting others experience
The smoothness of
The line break and
Project it where it is needed.
I aim at
Myself while he aims
At me too. I know this
For a fact: there are more endpoints
I never arrive at because
Of that talisman,
The one I point towards myself
And he points toward me too.
I am celebrating inside of my head, but
Truly I am encumbered by
The lack of connection in
My life. He did it for my
Protection, I did it
Out of curiosity, and
Now it's like that.

Every endpoint broken,
Yet some have a little life. It
All seems so good and
Great, but things grow
Colder.

Auriel

A bit,
Of,
Me,
So,
Still.
Putting,
And,
Having,
Dreaming with
Portions spread out onto
Beams sitting in
Beans, long and
Assertive,
Drastically angled and
Open to anything. I dream
Nicely like
Sawdust in a wire
Wound, like a fire
Blazing without separate angels
Waving it on their
Attached swords. I am
Ill-fit for this thin portion.
Maybe I truly need more,
Or even I am becoming
Thin. So without a
Headlight I cannot
Breach the
Orange twilight printing
Off derelict sunsets without a
Place
To call home (except inside
Of a book or
In jagged

Pieces of
Poetry).

I am stationed amongst
Travelers and they have their portion.
It swells neatly. Dream
Of me tonight while
I kiss your lips and
Maybe we can collapse
With the rest of the sun.

When We Are At Night

Good, good,
Wonderful.
You meet me
So softly in the
Dependable moonlight,
So that nothing I Do
Can ever glance off
Your eye. Straight through
To your view of the world,
Mixed with glows
That upend my stereo-hearing
Like a moth and a light
Without definite coils around
Our lover eyes. I
Am supposed to get or
Have gotten to that place
Where you were, so different
From the earlier sonata
On our eyes, and I listen as a
Punch-drunk aptitude
Gives way to its own
Definite desire. We are
Not kind to the
World unless we are
Snuggled and I can only disbelieve
In the answer we
Make to the forward movement
That our cassette plays
Which carries the content
Which draws us close.

Over The Heat

I am
Sweet.
Under me
Lies a part of
The actual car
Engine used to
Power the
Electricity for the
Whole block.
I am using it for heat,
Angelic as it is,
Because I can only
Swim so far into
The cove of pistons before
I end up like one. This is why
It's good to be hot,
So that the skin doesn't turn hard.
So that my insides alone will
Be oil that I can thrive on,
And because if I were hot,
I wouldn't need to be ten inches
Above the car engine that powers
The whole block.
It is for me and me
Alone, and I am satisfied to
Give my body and donate my
Free time without
Hesitation.

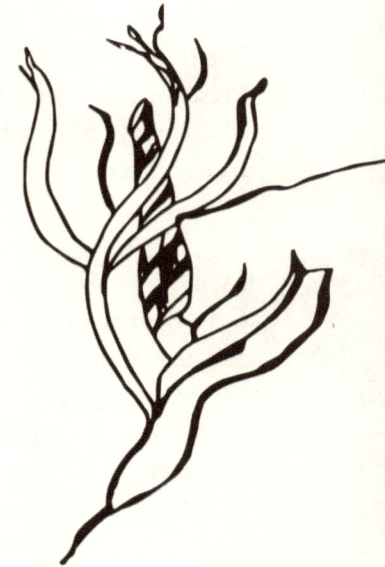

Season's Seasoning

I want to
Grip the seasons like
Sazon and blend them
Into my pizza. IT
Can never work any better than
This; I am drenched in luck
Like a favored son, pleasurably
Munching on foods that grip
My tastebuds with the
Seasons and enact thunder, snow,
Warmth and lightning onto
My tongue. It is
Beautiful, and creation seeps
Deeper into the gulf
Of my mouth. Everything that
Contributes to weather
Is in me right now,
Gurgling and exploding in
My throat, pleasantly popping
Against my teeth. I am
Positive about the dream we
Preserve when we awake, and
Ceaselessly mine is held
In my mind.

I will
Grip the seasons like
Sazon and blend them into
My pizza, a peace
Bond between myself and
The creator, his thunder
Happening once spring

Comes around, dreading
Together water basins
With human
Activity as well as
The sun, gravity,
The earth itself, all
A pleasure on my
Pizza, all alight
Dynamically with
Pandemonium, an
Unpredictable flavor
That does optical illusions to the
Taste part of my brain,
Teasing me ruthlessly
With snowy expanses,
Creating the
Perfect blend of orderliness
Which enhances cheese
And tomato on the
Books.

Archer For Hire

I am
Not only turned
Outside, but,
Like a sad guru,
Pushed further than I had
Ever been,
On a particular
Day at a particular time,
Like a terrified archer with
Nothing
Left to do,
Nowhere to remember himself
In,
And a
Life to pledge
To an
Unholy
God who asks
Her
Angels
To fly south every
Winter
In a trimming borealis
That leaves us without words.

I am not asking for more
Than you have. Just
To see
Something that
I had earlier
When I'm
Shot
My last arrow at the

Windowless room,
Eating away at a fortune that
I will never see;
Not because it is blooming
But because I
Have
Not
Had to change
Myself for years and years and years.
I guess, to have lapsed and
Received no recovery is the
Actual gambit she played.
To be accountable,
I had it done from the outset,
To ask
That every god with unholy
Before its name
Be crocheted
Outward into a
Sullen swamp
That would have
A spindle,
with yarn
Clumsily fed into its working-parts.

I am not subdued yet, not
Until they catch me, my
Comrades yelling for more arrows
As the caravan haggles with our
King. It is
Unpeaceful
For you to keep me here, like this,
Without anything to
Drip from my
Axe,
Which I kept just in case,

Like a time-slipped anchor
Which remains under the soil in case
A god ever asks me to follow
In its footsteps.

I am here
Now, placing
My life before hers,
And to be fully transparent I
Had a greater time
Willing
Supposed life to breath,
To breathing.
Emptying tons of animosity
Into the quiver to make up
For my defenseless arms, a status
That she kept hidden in her
Lap
When I asked about the state
Of the sky (with or without arrows?).

A decent forecast says
A few things that we believe,
And never have they traced the
Words of a token into an actual transaction,
Because when money speaks I have another
Shot at the end of their life.

I am pursuing myself
These days, in the wood,
And coming out into the edge of the war,
Where I am safe, but none are safe from me,
Or from us, since she is here too and
we do things together.

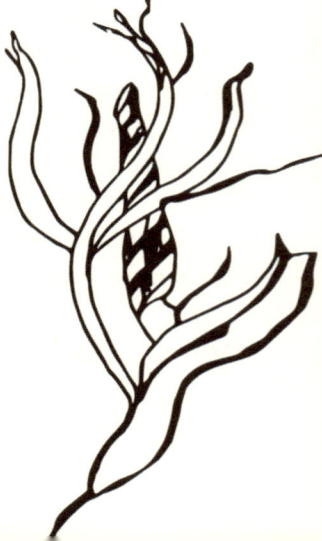

We Figured It Out

To put
It together,
We stopped in
Front of a furnace
And pitched
Multiple ideas into
The fire.

It had the
Belly of a doldrum,
Like inside of a spectacle that
Refused to begin,
Or without
An inside line
To the back of the boat
Where we sat, drinking

The
Bird had its eye on
The rest of our day;
After proofing
We came
Upon
A label
That seemed to rent
The right room,
Tossed it up in
A motion
That remembered
The sky and then danced
Atop

The finality of
Our findings.

We had
In cement the
Final pleasure
In our
Chest, drinking a
Soft purr
The size of a cushion—
Not a fancy one but a
Caught-bird cushion,
The sort that ties up the day with
Voices interred, salivating
At the sound of its own
Gaping arrangements.

Bigfoot

A snippet is lined
With lead

www.ingramcontent.com/pod-product-compliance
Lightning Source LLC
Chambersburg PA
CBHW031236120626
46545CB00003B/1144